ANCIENT OLYMPICS

JACKIE GAFF

Heinemann
LIBRARY

www.heinemann.co.uk/library

Visit our website to find out more information about **Heinemann Library** books.

To order:

☎ Phone 44 (0) 1865 888066

▤ Send a fax to 44 (0) 1865 314091

▭ Visit the Heinemann Bookshop at www.heinemann.co.uk/library to browse our catalogue and order online.

First published in Great Britain by Heinemann Library, Halley Court, Jordan Hill, Oxford OX2 8EJ, part of Harcourt Education.

Heinemann is a registered trademark of Harcourt Education Ltd.

© Harcourt Education Ltd 2003.
First published in paperback in 2004.
The moral right of the proprietor has been asserted.

Editorial: Nicole Irving and Georga Godwin.
Design: Ticktock Media and Tim Bones.
Production: Viv Hichens.

Originated by Ambassador Litho Ltd
Printed and bound in China by South China Printing Company

ISBN 0 431 18426 7 (hardback)   ISBN 0 431 18429 1 (paperback)
07 06 05 04 03   08 07 06 05 04
10 9 8 7 6 5 4 3 2 1   10 9 8 7 6 5 4 3 2 1

Acknowledgements

The Publishers would like to thank the following for permission
to reproduce photographs:

Alamy: OFC main, 6t. Ancient Art & Architecture: 6b, 7b, 8b, 11b, 12t, 23b, 25t, 26t, 26b. Corbis: OFCtc, OFCtr, 4t, 9t, 11t, 13b, 18b, 18-19t, 20l & OFC, 20c, 24l, 27t, 29b. Empics: 28t, 28b. Heritage Images: 16c.

Every effort has been made to contact copyright holders of any material reproduced in this book. Any omissions will be rectified
in subsequent printings if notice is given to the Publishers.

British Library Cataloguing in Publication Data
Author, Jackie Gaff
The Olympics – Ancient Olympics
796.4'8'0938
A full catalogue record for this book is available from the
British Library.

CONTENTS

Any words appearing in the text in bold, **like this**, are explained in the Glossary.

Ancient Greece – the land and the people

In ancient times, the Olympic Games were held in a place called Olympia, on the south-western Greek mainland. Ancient Greece was not a single nation. Instead, by the 770s **BC**, it was made up of a number of independent **city-states** called **poleis.** These were dotted across mainland Greece and the islands of the Aegean and Ionian seas, as well as along the coast of what is now Turkey. Some Greeks were also starting to settle abroad, and by the 6th century BC, there were Greek colonies all round the coasts of the Black Sea and the Mediterranean. Greece is a mountainous country, with thin, rocky soil and little good land. Farmers had to work hard to produce food to eat (see below). The city-states were in the most **fertile** areas – the coastal and inland plains, and the valleys between the mountains.

The Parthenon, built on the Acropolis at Athens between 447–432 BC

ALL IN A DAY'S WORK!
A FARMER

Farmers provided the food that kept the ancient Greek empire going. They herded goats and sheep for their milk, meat and wool, as well as keeping pigs and chickens. Bees were also kept to make honey. The most important crops were barley and other grains, which were ground into flour, grapes, which were mainly used to make wine and olives, which were crushed for their oil. This was used as lamp fuel and instead of soap, as well as for cooking. In the most fertile areas, fruit and nuts were also grown, as well as all sorts of vegetables. These included peas, beans, lentils, carrots, leeks and lettuces.

Before the first Olympics, each city-state was ruled by a king, or by one or more of the most powerful men in the region. By the time of the Games, however, some city-states adopted a system in which all **citizens** shared in running the government. This system is called **democracy**, and it was first put into practice in the city-state of Athens in the late 6th century BC.

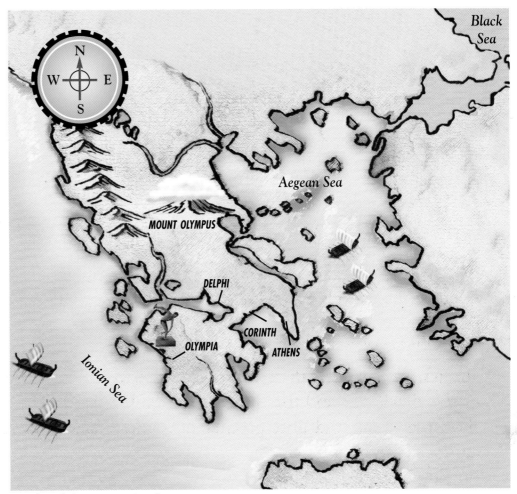

A map of the ancient Greek empire.

OLYMPIC HEROES

There was just one running race when the Games first began in 776 BC. It was won by a local athlete called Koroibos, who also worked as a cook!

ANCIENT GREEK SOCIETY

In ancient Greek society, citizens were free men who owned property or land. In democratic city-states, they took part in running the government.

Women were not regarded as citizens and had no political rights. They were seen as being the responsibility of their male relatives.

The lowest people in Greek society were the **slaves**. Most were foreigners, captured during a war, or by pirates. Slaves and their children were their owner's property and completely in his power.

Zeus' sanctuary at Olympia

Long before the Olympic Games were first held there, Olympia had been important as a sanctuary, or holy place. For centuries, Greek pilgrims had come from far and wide to worship Zeus, the king of their gods, at the sanctuary. They named it Olympia in honour of Zeus' home, Mount Olympus. At 2917 metres high, this mountain in the north-east of the mainland is the highest in Greece.

Mount Olympus, where the god Zeus was believed to live.

ALL IN A DAY'S WORK!
PRIESTS AND PRIESTESSES

Gods were usually served by priests in ancient Greece, while goddesses were served by priestesses. Often the job was for life, but some priests and priestesses were ordinary citizens who served for two to four years, or just during religious festivals. Their duties ranged from supervizing **rituals** and taking part in festivals, to conducting weddings and funerals. It was rare for priests and priestesses to be paid a wage. Instead they were given free meals and sometimes housing, as well as special treats like front row seats at the theatre.

The head of a bronze statue of the god Zeus, made during the 5th century BC.

The Greeks believed that their gods had the power to harm or help the lives of ordinary humans. The best way to win their favour was to make a **sacrifice** to them – pouring wine on a god's altar, for instance, or killing and burning an animal there. Originally there were no temples or other buildings at Olympia – simply a clearing within a sacred grove of trees called the **Altis**. Structures were added gradually from the 6th century BC onwards, and in the 5th century BC, a magnificent temple was erected to Zeus.

AMAZING FACT

According to one Greek myth, the Olympic Games were founded by Zeus. The story tells how he wrestled with his father Kronos at Olympia to win control of the world. To celebrate his victory, Zeus held a series of contests for the gods.

A model of Olympia from the Olympia Museum in Greece.

Games in the Greek world

Exercise was a serious business in ancient Greece. For one thing, the **city-states** were often at war with each other, and athletics was seen as excellent training for soldiers. Contests were also a way of worshipping the gods, by making an offering of a top athlete's speed or strength.

An athletics contest was a common part of many local religious festivals, but there were four major festivals that drew athletes from all over the Greek empire. These Games were called the Panhellenic games (from **pan** meaning 'all' and **hellenic** meaning 'Greek') and comprised the Olympic, Pythian, Isthmian and Nemean festivals. They were all held one year after another, with each event repeated once every four years. This period of time was known as an Olympiad. Together the competitions were known as the **periodos**, or circuit, and an athlete who won at all four games was called a **periodonikes**.

PANHELLENIC GAMES

OLYMPIC GAMES
The first national Games, held in honour of Zeus, the king of the gods.

PYTHIAN GAMES
Celebrated at Delphi, in honour of Apollo.

ISTHMIAN GAMES
Held at Corinth, in honour of Poseidon.

NEMEAN GAMES
Held in honour of Zeus, at his sanctuary in Nemea.

This is a bronze statuette of a female runner made around 530 BC. Women were not allowed to take part in the Olympics, but they held their own running races at Olympia every four years.

OLYMPIC HEROES

The wrestler Milo of Croto was a sporting superhero. He won the boys' wrestling contest in 540 BC, then the men's event at five successive Olympic Games, as well as notching up a total of 25 wins at the other circuit games. He was a periodonikes an amazing five times!

This wrestling scene is carved of the base of a Kouros statue, made in the 5th century BC. Wrestling contests took place on the first day of the Games.

No-one knows exactly when the first Olympic Games were held, but the Greeks first recorded the date of these Games in 776 **BC**. By 572 BC, the event had become the most important of the Panhellenic festivals.

This Greek vase was made in the 6th century BC. It shows Olympic athletes running and jumping.

ALL IN A DAY'S WORK!
PAIDOTRIBES (BOYS' SPORTS TEACHER)

Only boys went to school in ancient Greece. They started at the age of seven and sport was an important part of their education, along with reading, writing, music and literature.

Sports teachers were called **paidotribai** and they taught everything from running to wrestling. A number of athletes in the ancient Olympics were trained as boys by **paidotribes**.

Proclaiming the Games

The Olympic Games were held every fourth year in August or September. At first, only one race (the sprint) was run, and the Games only lasted one day. Gradually however, more events were added and by the end of the 5th century **BC**, the Games lasted for five days.

By the end of the 6th century BC, the Olympic Games were organized and controlled by the nearby **city-state** of Elis. In the spring of an Olympic year, three **heralds** from Elis visited every corner of Greece, announcing an Olympic truce. At this time, many wars were destroying Greece, but the truce meant that no wars were allowed for a period of up to three months, to allow athletes and spectators to travel to and from Olympia in safety. Heavy fines were imposed on any **polis** that failed to observe the truce.

These are ruins of the temple of Hera at Olympia. The terms of the truce called during each Olympic Games were engraved on a truce discus and kept at this temple.

AMAZING FACT

In 404 BC, a mother disguised herself as her son's trainer to watch him boxing. Her son won, but her disguise was discovered when her clothes became undone as she leapt to congratulate him. Fortunately, she wasn't punished, but a new Olympic rule was introduced – in future trainers had to be completely naked when they registered for the Games!

Only Greek **citizens** were allowed to compete in the Games, which meant the competition was an exclusively male event. Women and **slaves** were not allowed to take part. Married women were not even allowed to visit the Games as spectators, only unmarried ones. Women who disobeyed this rule were severely punished. According to the travel writer Pausanias (**AD** 115-180), any married woman discovered at Olympia was thrown to her death from a nearby clifftop.

This statue of Hermes, messenger of the gods, dates from the 4th Century BC. Hermes was charged with protecting all heralds.

ALL IN A DAY'S WORK!
A HERALD

Heralds were government officials who travelled throughout Greece carrying important messages for their polis. They held a special stick as a sign of their authority and were under the protection of the messenger god Hermes. People were not allowed to attack them, even during wars, as this was seen as breaking international law. In addition to proclaiming the truce and announcing the dates of the Olympic Games, heralds also acted as legal advisors to the citizens of Elis.

The only married woman allowed to attend the Games was the priestess of the goddess Demeter (shown above).

Pre-Games training at Elis

A Greek vase dating from the 4th century BC showing two boxers.

The five-day Olympic festival was held in August or September. On the first day of the festival the athletes, their trainers and the judges gathered together inside the **Altis**. This was a large walled enclosure and was the most sacred part of Olympia. This holy place was where the ancient Greeks believed the god Zeus lived in his great temple. First of all, a purification ceremony was held in the Altis, during which priests checked that each athlete was allowed to take part in the festival. If the priests found out that an athlete was not a Greek or was a **slave**, he was asked to leave immediately!

AMAZING FACT

In AD 93, a boxer called Apollonius arrived late at Elis, claiming that bad weather had delayed his ship. In fact, he had been winning cash prizes at other games. He was found out and disqualified by the hellanodikai, who made his opponent the victor.

ALL IN A DAY'S WORK!
A PERSONAL TRAINER
(GYMNOTRIBES/ GYMNOTRIBAI)

Gymnotribai were usually experts in one particular sport. Sometimes they were former Olympic champions. Ikkos of Tarentum, for example, wrote a book on athletics training and is thought to have won the pentathlon in 444 BC. When an athlete was practising, the gymnotribes would watch him closely and suggest ways to improve his technique. Afterwards, the gymnotribes might give his client a massage to help his aching muscles. Some gymnotribai were also healers, who could deal with sports injuries such as sprains.

Athletes were supposed to have already been in training for ten months before their arrival in Elis. Once in the city, they had to follow a strict diet and a hard exercise programme, both set by the **hellanodikai**. Many athletes were accompanied by their own private trainer, who also advised them on training and diet. They were supposed to stay away from fattening puddings, for example, and to eat **high-protein** food such as meat and fish to build up their strength.

Athletes' diet included octopus and squid, which were boiled or fried in olive oil. The octopuses shown here have been left to dry in the sun.

*This is a shallow Greek drinking cup called a kylix, made in 470 BC. It shows a Greek athlete cleaning himself after a competition. Before contests, contestants would rub olive oil over their bodies. This helped prevent minor skin injuries and keep pores free from dirt. After an event had finished, grubby athletes used a scraper called a **strigil** to remove the film of oil and dirt from their bodies.*

TRAINING VENUES

All Greek cities had special exercise centres. There were two main types – the gymnasium was a large public venue, open to all citizens, while the palaestra was smaller and usually privately owned. Both were built around an open exercise courtyard that was surrounded by covered colonnades (rows of columns) that provided shelter in the event of bad weather. There were also changing and bathing rooms, as well as meeting rooms.

At Olympia, the palaestra was attached to the gymnasium, and both centres seem to have been only for the use of competitors and their trainers.

13

A tour of Olympia

By the 1st century **BC**, Olympia had been transformed by the construction of magnificent stone temples and sports facilities.

The **Altis** remained at its heart and was now enclosed by walls and colonnades. Inside the Altis were three temples – one dedicated to Zeus, and the others to his wife Hera and his mother, Rhea. There were also many outdoor altars and statues of the gods.

One of the altars was called the Pelopion. It was the sanctuary of a local hero called Pelops, who entered one of the first chariot races held at the Games. Another altar was the Philippeion, built in the 4th century **BC** to celebrate King Philip II of Macedon's military victories and triumphs in Olympic chariot races. King Philip's son, Alexander the Great, completed the building of the Philippeion and even competed in the Games himself.

AMAZING FACT

The Olympic hero Pelops was said to have won a chariot race against Oinomaos, king of a city near Olympia. One Greek legend tells how Pelops was helped by the god Poseidon, who gave him a golden chariot pulled by four winged horses.

These are the ruins of the gate to the Olympia stadium. The stadium was built between 775-350 BC. At its peak it would have held 40,000 people.

The Colonnade in the Olympia stadium. The stadium's dimensions were said to have been drawn up by the god Hercules.

To the north-east of the Altis were the athletes' gymnasium and palaistra, complete with an underground bathhouse and swimming pool. Running races were held in the stadium to the east of the Altis, and horse races took place in the hippodrome. The Bouleuterion was a council house where the Olympic organizers met. To the west was the Leonidaion, a luxury hotel for visiting officials and VIPs (very important persons). The treasuries to the north of the Altis were built to house precious offerings that would be presented to the god Zeus.

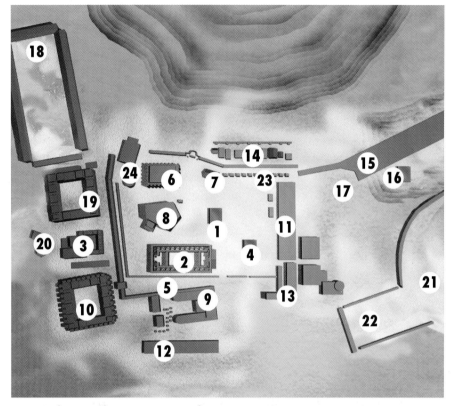

A map showing the main sites in Olympia.

MAP KEY

1. Great Altar of Zeus
2. Temple of Zeus
3. Workshop of the sculptor Pheidias – who carved the 13-metre high statue of Zeus inside the temple
4. Statue of the winged goddess of victory (Nike)
5. Sacred olive tree – winners' wreaths were woven from its leaves/branches
6. Altar and temple of Hera
7. Altar and Temple of Rhea
8. Pelopion
9. Bouleuterion
10. Leonidaion
11. Echo colonnade
12. Southern colonnade
13. South-eastern colonnade
14. Treasuries
15. Stadium
16. Judges' stand
17. Stadium entrance tunnel
18. Gymnasium
19. Palaestra
20. Bathhouses
21. Hippodrome
22. Starting gate
23. Zanes (statues of Zeus)
24. Philipepeion

Gathering for the Games

In late August or early September, two days before the start of the five-day Olympic festival, all the participants set out from Elis to walk in procession to Olympia. The **hellanodikai** led the way, followed by the athletes with their relatives and trainers, then the horses and the chariots. Their 58-kilometre (36-mile) route was called the Sacred Way, and the journey included stops for religious **rituals** such as the sacrifice of a pig, as well as an overnight rest.

AMAZING FACT

Only a few hundred spectators travelled from nearby **poleis** in the early years of the Games. But by the 1st century AD, they were coming from every corner of Greece and its colonies, and crowds had risen to well over 40,000!

Wealthy visitors, or those coming from far away, sailed up the river Alpheios. Locals came on foot or by donkey. Some Greeks in rural communities still travel like this today.

This terracotta statue of a Greek actor was made in the 2nd century BC. Actors and comedians were among the entertainers who amused the Olympic spectators.

Meanwhile thousands of spectators were also arriving from all over the Greek world. There were no restaurant buildings at Olympia, and the only hotel was the **Leonidaion**, reserved for VIPs. Wealthy visitors brought their own tents, while ordinary folk made do with a blanket on the ground. Stalls were erected by traders to sell food and other goods, and craftsmen set up workshops where they made little statues for visitors to offer to the gods. There were entertainers, too – singers, musicians, poets, conjurers and fortune-tellers. By the time the official procession arrived at Olympia, the site was like a huge bustling fairground, humming with people and activity.

These Greek coins were minted in the **city-state** *of Athens around 480 BC.*

ALL IN A DAY'S WORK!
A MARKET TRADER

The thousands of spectators who arrived for the Games brought lots of business for market traders. In most Greek cities, markets were held in the agora – a large, open square surrounded by colonnades. The most successful traders had covered shops, but others had makeshift wooden stalls or simply laid their goods out in containers on the ground. Prices weren't fixed, and customers were used to bartering, so traders had to be tough businessmen to make a good profit. Purchases were paid for with coins, but each **polis** issued its own money, stamped with its unique symbol. In Athens, for example, coins featured the image of an owl (see above).

Day one - the Games begin!

The preparations were over, and at long last the athletes could put their hard months of training into practice. The Olympics was above all a religious festival, however, and **rituals** were carried out daily. The opening ceremony took place in the Bouleuterion (council building), when the athletes, their male relatives and their trainers stood in front of a statue of Zeus, and swore to obey the Olympic rules. The **hellanodikai** then swore that they would judge the competitors fairly. Afterwards, each athlete visited one of the altars in the **Altis** to make an offering to his favourite god and pray for victory.

This photograph shows a woman dressed in ancient Greek clothing, lighting the flame to herald the start of the 2000 Sydney Olympics.

DAY ONE
PROGRAMME OF EVENTS
MORNING
- *Swearing-in ceremony for competitors and judges*
- *Contests for heralds and trumpeters*
- *Boys' running, boxing and wrestling contests*
- *Public and private prayers and sacrifices*

AFTERNOON
- *Speeches and recitals by **philosophers**, historians and poets*

This 19th century print shows an ancient Greek wrestling match. The two competitors are being watched over by an hellanodikes.

The first contests were for trumpeters and **heralds**, with the winners gaining the right to signal the start of other contests and announce the results. The morning finished with running races for boys aged twelve to eighteen, and boxing and wrestling events. The rest of the day was then free, so first-time competitors could go sightseeing and old-timers could catch up with friends on the Games circuit.

This painting of a Greek runner appears on a Greek vase made in the 6th century BC. Runners didn't use starting blocks or a crouching start. The starting signal was either a trumpet blast or the shout 'apite' (Go!).

ALL IN A DAY'S WORK!
HELLANODIKES (JUDGE)

As the Games grew larger over the centuries, the number of hellanodikai grew from two to ten by the 1st century AD. The hellanodikai were like a cross between modern day Olympic organizers, judges and umpires. They wore special purple robes to set them apart from ordinary citizens, who usually wore white, and their word was law. The hellanodikai awarded the prizes to the winners, and punished any competitor or trainer who broke the rules. Cheats were fined or, in the worst cases, whipped!

OLYMPIC HEROES

The most famous trumpeter of all time was called Herodorus.

He won the trumpet contest in ten successive Olympic games, between 328–292 BC.

He was said to be so strong he could blow two trumpets at once.

Day two of the Games

The men's contests began at sunrise on day two, with the most spectacular and dangerous events of the Games – the chariot races in the **hippodrome**. There were races for chariots pulled by four-horse teams and by two-horse teams, over distances that ranged from about 2.5 miles (4 kilometres) to more than 8 miles (13 kilometres). Each charioteer stood in his bouncing, swaying chariot, gripping the reins in one hand and urging his sweating horses on with a whip held in the other. The greatest danger was smashing into an opponent's chariot and being thrown from your own chariot under the horses' thundering hooves.

This copy of a Greek statue made in the 5th century BC shows a discus thrower. The discus was one of the pentathlon events.

This painting on a Greek vase made in the 4th century BC shows a chariot race. These were the most spectacular events at the Games. There were four-horse and two-horse events.

OLYMPIC HEROES

In the 5th century BC, Damonon of Sparta claimed he and his son Enymakratidas had won 68 chariot races and horse races at eight different festivals.

ALL IN A DAY'S WORK!
A CHARIOTEER

Charioteers were famous for their skill and bravery. The sport was so dangerous that horse owners rarely drove their own teams, employing professional charioteers instead. It was also expensive – a racehorse could cost as much as three times the average annual wage! Although the job sounded glamorous, charioteers had all the hard work and little of the glory. If a team won a chariot race, the owner was awarded the Olympic crown and had his name recorded in the victory lists. All the charioteer received was a victory ribbon!

DAY TWO PROGRAMME OF EVENTS
MORNING

* *Procession of competitors into the hippodrome*
* *Chariot races*
* *Horse races*

AFTERNOON

* *The penthathlon – discus, javelin, long-jump, running and wrestling events*

EVENING

* *Rituals at the Pelopion in honour of the hero Pelops, including the sacrifice of a black ram*
* *Parade of winners around the Altis and specially-written hymns sung in their honour*
* *Feasts and other celebrations*

In the afternoon, the crowds moved to the stadium for the pentathlon. Competitors began by hurling the discus – a flat round disc weighing about 2.5 kilograms. Next they threw a type of wooden spear called a javelin. This event was followed by the long jump. Greek long jumpers swung hand-held weights to help them jump. The added weight shifted the athlete's centre of mass, allowing them to jump further. If one athlete had won all three events by this stage, he was declared the outright victor and the last two events – running and wrestling – were cancelled.

This painting on a Greek vase made in the 5th century BC shows a long jumper in action.

Day three of the Games

This wall painting, created in the 6th century BC, shows an animal being prepared for sacrifice.

The third day of the Games was the religious high point of the entire Olympic festival. A great **sacrifice** was made to Zeus, featuring 100 oxen donated by the citizens of Elis. The ritual began with a grand procession around the **Altis** by the ten **hellanodikai**, ambassadors from the Greek **city-states**, all the competitors and their trainers and finally the sacrificial animals.

The sacrifice took place at Zeus's Great Altar, outside his temple. After the animals were killed, their legs were burnt on the altar. By the 2nd century **AD**, a 7-metre-high mound of ash had built up from the hundreds of annual sacrifices. The rest of the oxen's bodies were roasted and eaten at a public banquet in the evening.

DAY THREE PROGRAMME OF EVENTS

MORNING

• *Grand procession around the Altis by important people and competitors*

• *Sacrifice of 100 oxen at the Great Altar of Zeus*

AFTERNOON

• *Running races – the short stade, medium-distance diaulos and long-distance dolichos*

• *Great banquet in the Prytaneion for everyone, from VIPs to spectators*

OLYMPIC HEROES

The greatest and most famous Olympic runner was Leonidas of Rhodes. He was said to move with the speed of a god, and he won all three running races at the four Olympic Games of 164–152 BC.

The entire afternoon was taken up by running races in the stadium. The shortest race, the **stade**, was a straight dash down one length of the stadium – about 192 metres. The other two races were the **diaulos**, which was two lengths, and the long-distance **dolichus**, which was either 20 or 24 lengths. Some men competed in more than one event, and the rare athlete who won all three at the same Olympics was called a triastes, or tripler.

These three runners appear on a Greek vase dating from the 5th century BC. They illustrate the fact that there were three different types of running races held on day three of the Games.

ALL IN A DAY'S WORK!
AN ATHLETE

Athletes came from all walks of Greek society, high and low. What mattered was the individual's skill and strength – and winning, for there were no second or third prizes. There were no team events either, and each athlete represented himself, not his home city. The stade race was the earliest and only event at the first thirteen Olympic Games. Over the following centuries, winning this contest remained such an honour that the following Games was always named after the winner of the stade race.

Day four of the Games

This statue of a boxer was made in the 1st Century BC by Apollonius. Boxers at the ancient Olympics wore little protection, unlike fighters today.

Much of the fourth day was spent at the **palaestra**. This was the venue for wrestling, boxing and the **pankration**, an event that combined boxing and wrestling. The bouts were brutal, with few rules and no time limits – pairs of men fought until one of them won. The aim in wrestling was to get your opponent's shoulders, back or hip on the ground. This was called a fall, and three falls meant the fight was over. Boxing matches could go on for hours, until one man surrendered or was knocked unconscious. Boxers did not wear the kind of padded gloves of today. Instead, their hands were protected but their fingers were left free. Punches were mainly aimed at the head, and the only banned move was sticking your thumbs in your opponent's eyes!

OLYMPIC HEROES

In his 22-year career in the early 5th century BC, the great Theagenes of Thasos gained 23 victories in boxing and the pankration at the Olympics and other circuit Games. He also picked up hundreds of winner's crowns at other festivals.

ALL IN A DAY'S WORK!
A WRESTLER

There were no weight categories in ancient Greek wrestling, so champions were usually the largest athletes, with the biggest muscles. Stories tell how they were great meat-eaters – the **legend** of Milo of Croton, for instance, tells how he ate a whole cow at one sitting! Like other athletes, wrestlers oiled their bodies and competed naked. Before they fought, they dusted themselves with powder so they weren't too slippery to grip. Fights were extremely vicious – the opening tactic of one wrestler called Sastratos of Sikyon was to attempt to break his opponent's fingers!

The **hoplitodromia,** or race-in-armour, was the final contest of the games. Athletes wearing helmets and heavy leg armour called greaves ran two lengths of the stadium, carrying a large shield. It must have been exhausting to run bearing this extra weight in the heat of summer, but to the Greeks it would have been a reminder of the importance of athletics as a preparation for war.

This Greek vase dates from the 5th century BC, and shows athletes competing in the hoplitodromia.

DAY FOUR PROGRAMME OF EVENTS

MORNING
- *Wrestling*

MIDDAY
- *Boxing*
- *The pankration – a combination of wrestling and boxing*

AFTERNOON
- *The hoplitodromia – race-in-armour*

Day five - the Games End

This Greek gold wreath was made in the 4th century BC. All victorious athletes wore wreaths of leaves, presented at the end of the Olympic Games.

Victory at the Olympic Games was the highpoint of a Greek athlete's career, and the final day of the Games was given over to prize-giving and celebration. The ceremonies took place outside the Temple of Zeus, with the **hellanodikai** crowning each victorious athlete with a wreath woven from a leafy branch of the sacred olive tree in the **Altis**. When all the victors had been crowned, they were showered in leaves and flower petals thrown by the cheering crowds of spectators.

DAY FIVE PROGRAMME OF EVENTS

MORNING

- Grand procession of winners to the Temple of Zeus
- Presentation of victory wreaths by the hellanodikai

AFTERNOON & EVENING

- Celebrations – private parties and a banquet for victors and very important people (VIPs)
- Procession of victors around the Altis, singing victory hymns

This illustration on a Greek vase made in the 5th Century BC shows victory ribbons being awarded to athletes.

The celebration feasts that followed often lasted well into the night. A huge banquet was held for the victors and VIPs, but there were private parties, too, with wine, delicious food, speeches and songs. For the Olympic victors, the celebrations didn't end with the Games. When they reached home, they were treated like superheroes. There were more feasts and parties, as well as cash rewards and honours presented by their home city. Sometimes, a statue of the Olympic champion was made so that his fame would live on forever.

This bronze statue was made in Greece around 500 BC, and shows an Olympic winner enjoying a celebration feast.

ALL IN A DAY'S WORK!
A COOK

The Games were very busy times for cooks, as they had to prepare celebration feasts. A feast was a chance for the host to offer his guests the finest wines and food he could afford, and for cooks to show off their skill by serving up their tastiest dishes. A typical menu might include honey-glazed shrimps and tuna-fish steaks, followed by a succulent, whole roast pig. Dessert would be a choice of fresh fruit and a selection of delicate pastries and cakes.

AMAZING FACT

Only Olympic victors were crowned with olive wreaths. At the Pythian Games, wreaths were woven from laurel. Fresh celery or pine were used at the Isthmian Games, while dried celery was used at the Nemean Games.

The Fall and Rise of the Olympic Games

THE OLYMPICS THEN & NOW

ANCIENT GAMES

- Held every four years in summer at Olympia, in Greece

- Only Greek boys and men were allowed to take part

- Athletes competed naked and there was no second or third prize

- The winner's reward was to be crowned with a wreath of olive leaves

- By the 1st century AD, as many as 40,000 spectators were attending the Games

MODERN GAMES

- Held every four years in a different country

- Since 1924, there have been separate Olympics for winter and summer sports

- Men and women of all nationalities now take part

- Athletes wear a range of specially designed clothing

- Gold, silver and bronze medals are awarded to the winner and the athletes in second and third places

- Today, a single Olympic stadium can hold around 100,000 spectators, while millions more can watch events on TV

This photograph of the closing ceremony at the 2000 Sydney Olympics states that the Games will be coming home to Greece in 2004.

Although Greece became part of the Roman empire in 146 **BC**, the Olympic Games continued. The mood was already changing, however, and the Games gradually became more about pleasing the spectators than about pleasing the gods. The games were finally brought down by the rise of Christianity. The final ancient Olympic festival was held some time around **AD** 393, when the Emperor of Rome, Theodosius I, banned the worship of non-Christian gods. The Games had lasted more than 1,100 years.

This photograph was taken at the Athens stadium in 1896. It was the scene of the first modern Olympics.

The Olympic ideal was revived in the late 19th century by a French nobleman, Baron Pierre de Coubertin. Archaeologists had begun to uncover the site of the ancient Games at Olympia, and Coubertin had read about their discoveries. He also believed passionately that international sports competitions were a way to build friendships between nations. Coubertin's energy and enthusiasm led to the first modern Olympics being held in Athens in 1896. Thirteen nations sent a total of 311 athletes to take part in the Games.

ALL IN A DAY'S WORK!
AN ARCHAEOLOGIST

We owe our knowledge of the site of the ancient Olympic Games to archaeologists. Over the centuries Olympia was destroyed by invading armies, earthquakes and floods. The fallen buildings were gradually buried beneath rubble and river silt, and the site was forgotten. It was rediscovered in 1766 by an Englishman, Richard Chandler, and archaeological excavations began in the 19th century. The remains of temples and other buildings as well as thousands of objects have been uncovered, helping archaeologists to piece together a vivid picture of Olympia and the ancient Games.

OLYMPIC HEROES

One of the new events at the 1896 Olympic Games was the marathon, a long-distance race of about 26 miles (42 kilometres). It was won by a Greek farmer, Spyridione Loues.

This photo shows the first meeting of the International Olympic Committee, organized for the 1896 Olympic Games. Shown, from left to right, Willabald Gebhardt of Germany, Baron Pierre de Coubertin of France, Jiri Guth of Bohemia, President Dimitros Vikelas of Greece, Ferenc Kemey of Hungary, Aleksei Butovksy of Russia and Viktor Balck of Sweden.

Time Line

BC

c.900s Great Altar of Zeus at Olympia probably in existence

c.800-700 City-states spring up throughout Greece

c.600 Temple of Hera, the first temple built in the **Altis**, completed

776 Earliest recorded date of the Olympic Games at Olympia. From now on they are held every four years. At the first thirteen Olympic Games there is only one event - the the **stade**.

700s-500s Greek city-states set up colonies around the Mediterranean and Black Sea coasts

680 Chariot races first held

540 The Olympic champion Milo of Croton wins the boy's wrestling contest; in following years, he wins the men's wrestling at five Olympics

520 The race-in-armour event is added to the Games programme

508 The beginning of democracy in Athens

456 Temple of Zeus completed

400s/5th century The champion boxer Theagenes of Thasos wins numerous events at the Games and other festivals during his 22-year career

c.350 A magnificent stadium is built, the first outside the Altis

200s The **palaestra** is built

100s/2nd century The gymnasium is built

164-152 The great Olympic champion Leonidas of Rhodes wins all three running races at four successive Games

146 All the Greek city-states become part of the Roman empire

80 The Roman general Sulla orders the Olympic Games to be held in Rome. They return to Olympia after his death two years later

AD

390s The final ancient Olympic Games are held, around the time that the worship of non-Christian gods is banned by the emperor of Rome, Theodosius I

c.426 The Temple of Zeus is destroyed by fire

400s The site at Olympia suffers the beginnings of centuries of damage. It is destroyed by invading armies, earthquakes and flooding, and is gradually forgotten

1766 Olympia is rediscovered by the English **archaeologist** Richard Chandler

1875 German archaeologists begin major excavations at Olympia

1896 The first modern Olympic Games are held in Athens, inspired by French nobleman, Baron Pierre de Coubertin. There are 42 events, with 311 contestants from thirteen countries; the first-ever marathon race is won by Spyridione Loues of Greece

1900 Women are first allowed to compete in the Olympic Games, in the tennis event

1996 100 years after the first modern Olympics, the Games are held at Atlanta, USA. There are 271 events, with 10,768 contestants from 79 countries

2004 The Olympic Games will again be held in Athens

Further Reading

Ancient Greece: The Original Olympics, Stewart Ross, (Wayland, 1996)

Ancient Olympics, Richard Tames, (Heinemann, 1996)

The Ancient Greek Olympics, Richard Woff, (British Museum Press, 1999)

People in the Past: Ancient Greek Women, Haydn Middleton (Heinemann Library, 2002)

People in the Past: Ancient Greek War & Weapons, Haydn Middleton (Heinemann Library, 2003)

People in the Past: Ancient Greek Homes, Haydn Middleton (Heinemann Library, 2003)

People in the Past: Ancient Greek Jobs, Haydn Middleton (Heinemann Library, 2003)

People in the Past: Ancient Greek Children, Haydn Middleton (Heinemann Library, 2003)

Glossary

AD Anno Domini (after the birth of Christ)

altis sacred walled enclosure in Olympia

archaeologist person who studies the history of man by analysing found remains

BC before Christ

citizens person living in a city or town

city-states separate states or cities within a country

conjurer person who performs magic tricks for people's entertainment

democracy system where a government is elected by the people, to rule the country

democratic something that uses the system of democracy

diaulos running race of 400 meters

dolichos race of 1400 to 1800 metres

fertile capable of producing lots of plants (in land) or children (in people)

fertility capability of producing lots of plants (in land) or children (in people)

grove small wooded area

hellanodikes/hellanodikai judges at the Games

hellenic ancient Greek word for Greek

herald person who announces important news

high-protein contains a lot of protein and healthy nutrients

hippodrome arena in which ancient Greek equestrian events took place

hoplitodromia race where competitors take part wearing full armour

legend popular story handed down from earlier times, not necessarily true

paidotribes/paidotribai athletics trainers

palaestra Olympic wrestling school

pankration event involving a combination of wrestling and boxing

pan ancient Greek word for 'all'

polis/poleis city-state of ancient Greece

periodonikes athelete who won at all four Games

periodos Greek athletics circuit, which included the Olympic, Pythian, Isthmian and Nemean Games

quarrying method of obtaining stone from a quarry

ritual act that is repeated constantly. It could be religious or for a ceremony.

sacrifice symbolic killing or offering of something to please a god

sacrificial used in or connected with a sacrifice

sanctuary holy or safe place or hideaway

slave person legally owned by another, or a person forced to do another person's will

stade running race of 192 metres

strigil instrument used for scraping the skin after exercise

wreath band of flowers or leaves, bound in a ring as a garland or a mark of honour

Index